RUSSIA COLORING BOOK

8 FAMOUS RUSSIAN LANDMARKS FOR COLORING

ARTHUR BENJAMIN

This page intentionally left blank.

ABOUT THE BOOK

Explore Russia's greatest landmarks through this coloring book. From enigmatic St. Basil's Cathedral to the majestic Peterhof Palace, this book is perfect for any lover of Russian culture.

Printed in the United States of America
ISBN: 978-1619495388

CONTENTS

This page intentionally left blank.

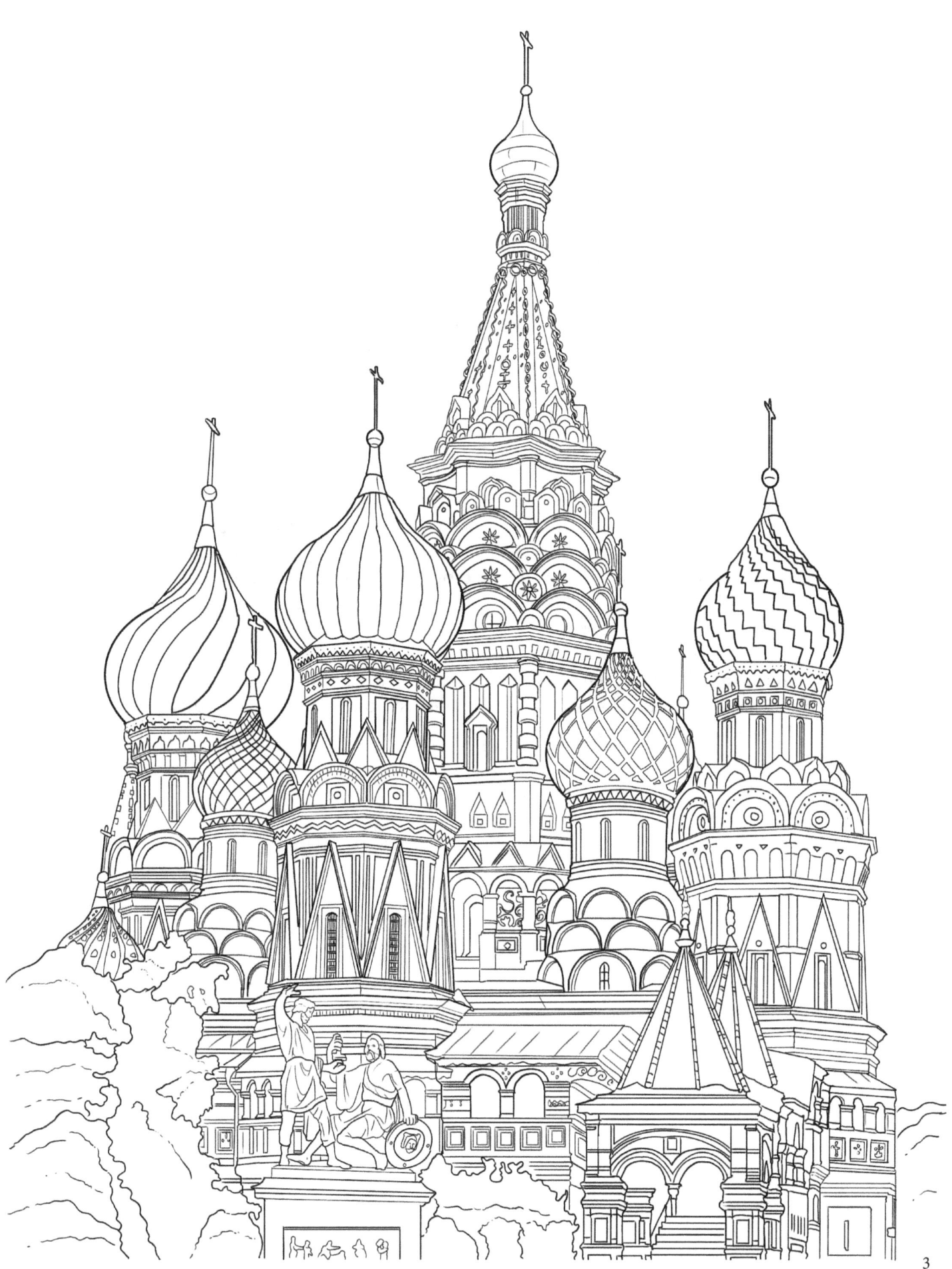

Plate 1.
St. Basil's Cathedral

St. Basil's Cathedral is probably one of the most recognizable buildings in the world. It was commissioned by Tsar Ivan the Terrible to commemorate the 1552 capture of Kazan from Mongol forces. It is officially called "The Cathedral of the Intercession of the Most Holy Theotokos on the Moat" or "Pokrovsky Cathedral" but owes its unofficial name to Basil the Blessed, a "holy fool-for-Christ" who was buried on the site a few years before the cathedral was erected.

The construction of the building was finished in 1961 and its design had absolutely no equivalent in either Russian or world architecture; its interior was rich with painted walls and the finest icons. Legend has it that once the work was complete, Ivan the Terrible ordered its creators, architects Barma and Postnik to be blinded so that they would not be able to recreate the beauty and grandeur of the masterpiece.

The building has a very unusual layout: it comprises eight side churches built around the ninth, central church of Intercession, with a tenth church added in 1588. The cathedral was initially white with golden domes and acquired its present-day, vivid colors in the 19th century.

After the Russian Revolution, St. Basil's Cathedral was desanctified and became a museum. There was even talk of demolishing it, but luckily this plan was never executed. The building has been part of the Moscow Kremlin and Red Square UNESCO World Heritage Site since 1990.

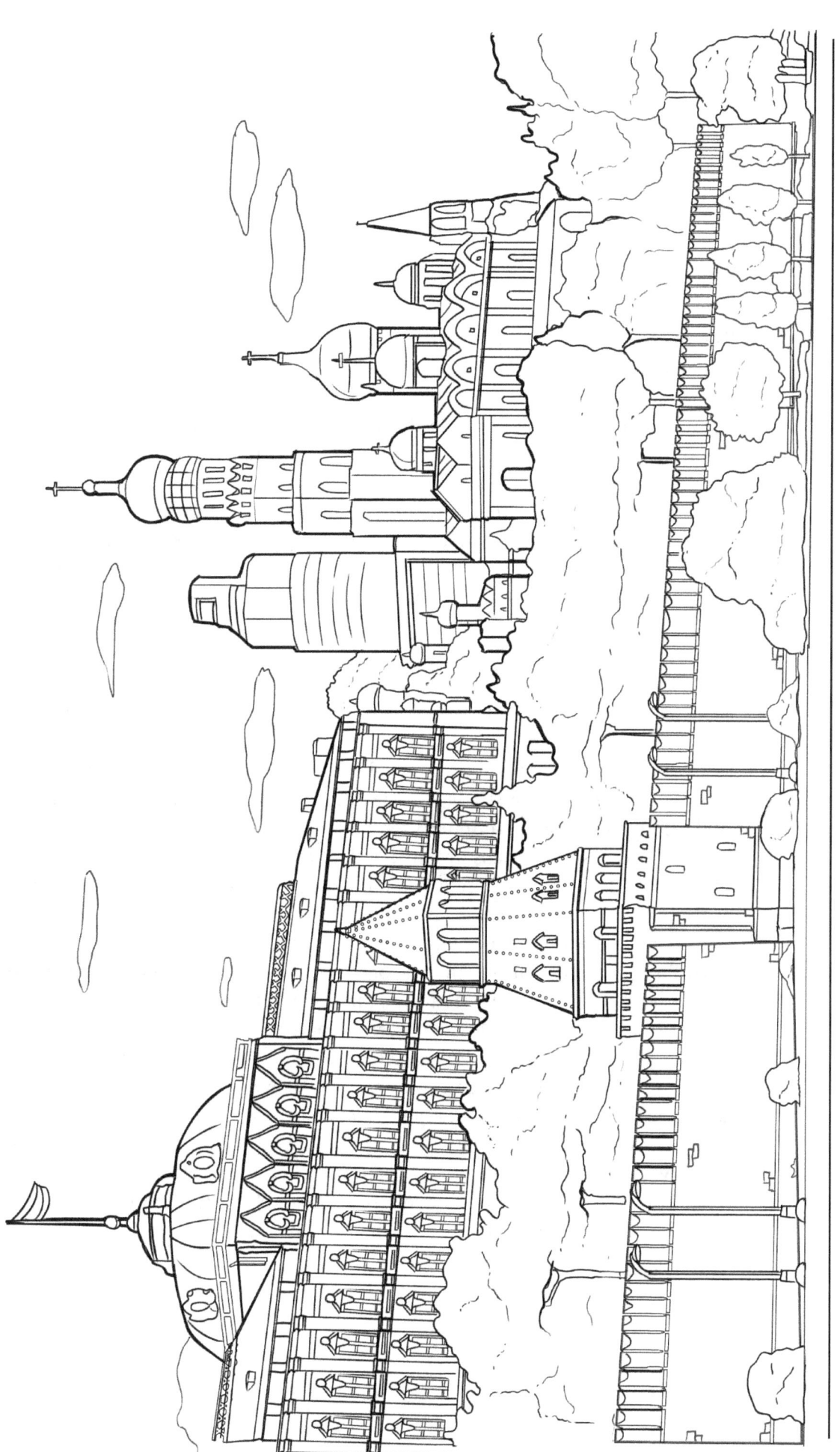

Plate 2.
The Kremlin

The Moscow Kremlin is a fortified 68-acre complex at the heart of Moscow. This remarkable group of buildings is not only one of the most impressive museums in the world but also the official residence of the President of the Russian Federation.

Its history, inseparable from the history of Moscow and Russia itself, starts in 1156, when the first wooden fort was built by Yuri Dolgoruki, Grand Duke of Kiev, on the site where the present-day Kremlin stands. After the wooden walls were repeatedly destroyed by fire during the 14th century, a decision was made to replace them with white limestone walls. The whole city of Moscow gradually grew around the Kremlin, which remained the very heart of it being the residence of the country's sovereigns.

It wasn't until the 15th century that the present day walls and most of the towers were erected; they were designed by a group of Italian architects under the reign of Ivan the Great. During that period, the Kremlin became the center of a unified Russian state; most of its cathedrals were constructed then, including the magnificent Cathedrals of the Assumption, the Annunciation and the Archangel. Another impressive addition to the Kremlin's skyline was Ivan the Great Bell Tower.

Moscow ceased to be the capital in 1712, when Peter the Great moved the government to Saint Petersburg, but even during that period the traditional ceremony of the coronation was held in the Kremlin's Annunciation Cathedral.

The space inside the walls was further developed and adapted by many generations of rulers, with more greatly significant buildings being added to the complex, such as the Kremlin Arsenal, the Senate Building and the Great Kremlin Palace.

After the Russian Revolution, Moscow once again became the capital, and the Kremlin regained its status as the seat of the country's government. The Soviet legacy can be seen in the large ruby-red stars that top many of the towers as well as in the modern architectural style of State Kremlin palace.

The present-day Kremlin is one of Russia's major tourist attractions. Visitors come to see its opulent cathedrals and churches, the enormous Tsar Bell and Tsar Cannon as well as the exterior of the Presidential Residence. Amongst other highlights is the Armoury Museum that has State Regalia, coronation dresses, carriages, Russian gold and silver artwork and armor on display. Another must-see is the Diamond Fund, boasting an unparalleled collection of gems and jewelry including The Great Imperial Crown of Catherine the Great adorned with 5000 diamonds.

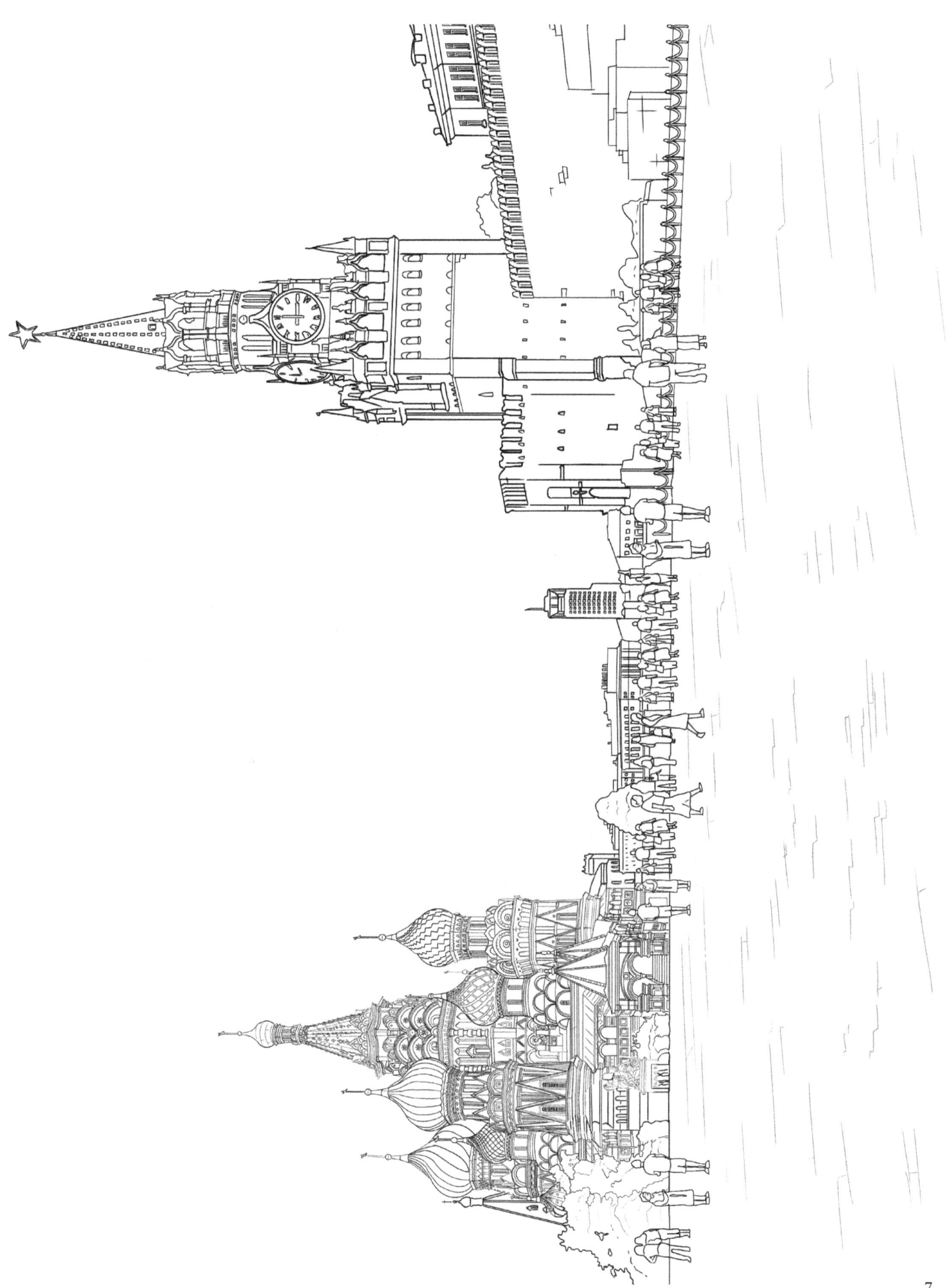

Plate 3.
Red Square

Situated next to the Kremlin, Red Square has been the heart and soul of the Russian capital for centuries. Contrary to a popular misconception, its name has nothing to do with Communism or the color of the Kremlin's wall that adjoins it. In fact, it originates from the Russian word 'krasnyi' which used to mean 'beautiful' before acquiring its contemporary meaning, 'red'.

The history of Red Square dates back to the 15th century. Ever since that time it has served as a meeting place as well as a marketplace for Muscovites. It has witnessed countless large gatherings, demonstrations, speeches and even executions. Among its most significant buildings are St. Basil's Cathedral, the State Historical Museum and the GUM Department Store, as well as the Lenin's Mausoleum, a modernist granite construction on the western edge of the square containing the remains of Vladimir Ilyich Lenin. In the Soviet era, people from all over the country would queue up for hours to see the embalmed body of the legendary leader of the Russian Revolution.

Built on Red Square in the 16th century, St. Basil's Cathedral is a world-famous landmark. The colorful building is shaped as bonfire flames rising into the sky. Although it has been a museum since the 1920s, one religious service a year is now held in the cathedral, in October, on the Day of Intercession.

In front of St. Basil's Cathedral is the monument to Minin and Pozharsky, the oldest monument in Moscow, erected in 1818 to commemorate the 1612 Russian victory over Polish invaders.

The State Historical Museum, situated opposite St. Basil's Cathedral, is one of the biggest museums in Moscow, with exhibits that range from relics of prehistoric tribes to priceless artworks that used to belong to the members of the Romanov dynasty.

In the course of the 20th century Red Square was used as a site for large Soviet military parades, the Mausoleum usually serving as a reviewing stand for the government leaders. There was even an idea to demolish St. Basil's Cathedral because it stood in way of the parades, but this plan was never carried out.

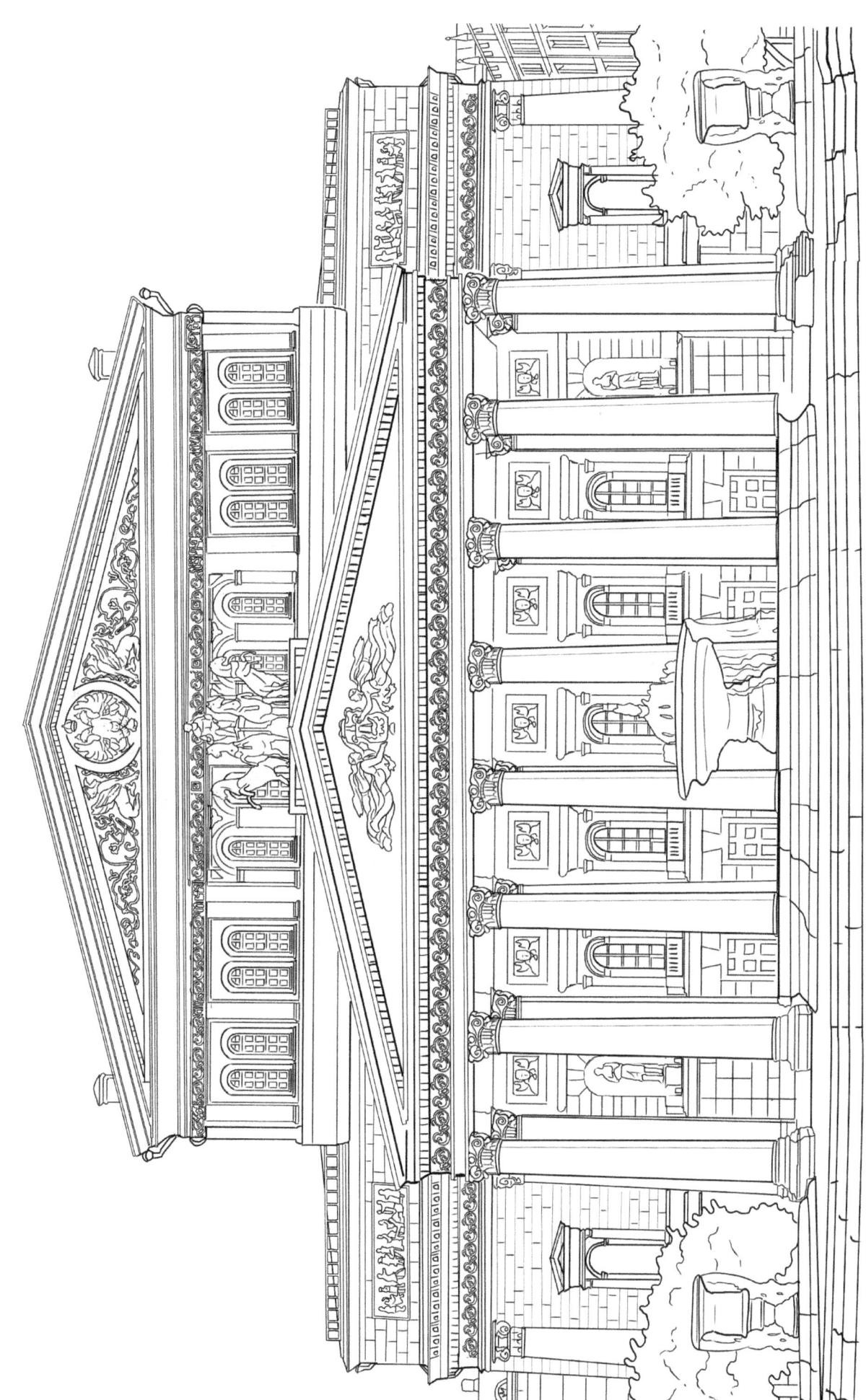

Plate 4.
Bolshoi Theatre

Moscow's Bolshoi Theatre is considered to be one of the greatest theatres in the world. It is the second biggest opera house in Europe, after La Scala in Milan.

The Company of the Bolshoi was originally founded in 1776 by Prince Peter Urusov and an English impresario, Michael Maddox, as "The Moscow Public Theatre." Moscow used to have only two theatres, one intended for opera and ballet and the other one for drama. Opera and ballet were considered to be more noble than drama so the opera house was named *Bolshoi*, meaning "grand" or "big", and the drama theater was called *Maly*, meaning "small." The company occupied various buildings until the present-day elegant theatre, designed by Joseph Bové, opened in 1856. The construction features the famous "Quadriga" — a statue of Apollo riding a four-horse chariot — created by Pyotr Klodt.

The Bolshoi Ballet and Bolshoi Opera are amongst the oldest and most celebrated ballet and opera companies in the world.

The Bolshoi is a repertory theatre — each season it presents a number of opera and ballet productions, performed in rotation.

Many of the world's greatest ballets premiered at the Bolshoi Theatre, such as Tchaikovsky's "Swan Lake" and Munkus's "Don Quixote". Other gems of the theatre's repertoire include Tchaikovsky's "The Sleeping Beauty" and "The Nutcracker", Adam's "Giselle", Prokofiev's "Romeo and Juliet" and Khachaturian's "Spartacus."

The Bolshoi has been the site of many renowned Russian opera performances, such as Mussorgsky's "Boris Godunov", Glinka's "A Life for the Tsar", and Rimsky-Korsakov's "The Tsar's Bride"; the theatre's stage has seen a number of important premiers including Tchaikovsky's "Voyevoda" and "Mazeppa", and Rachmaninoff's "Aleko" and "Francesca da Rimini". Operas by western, especially Italian, composers have also been regularly performed.

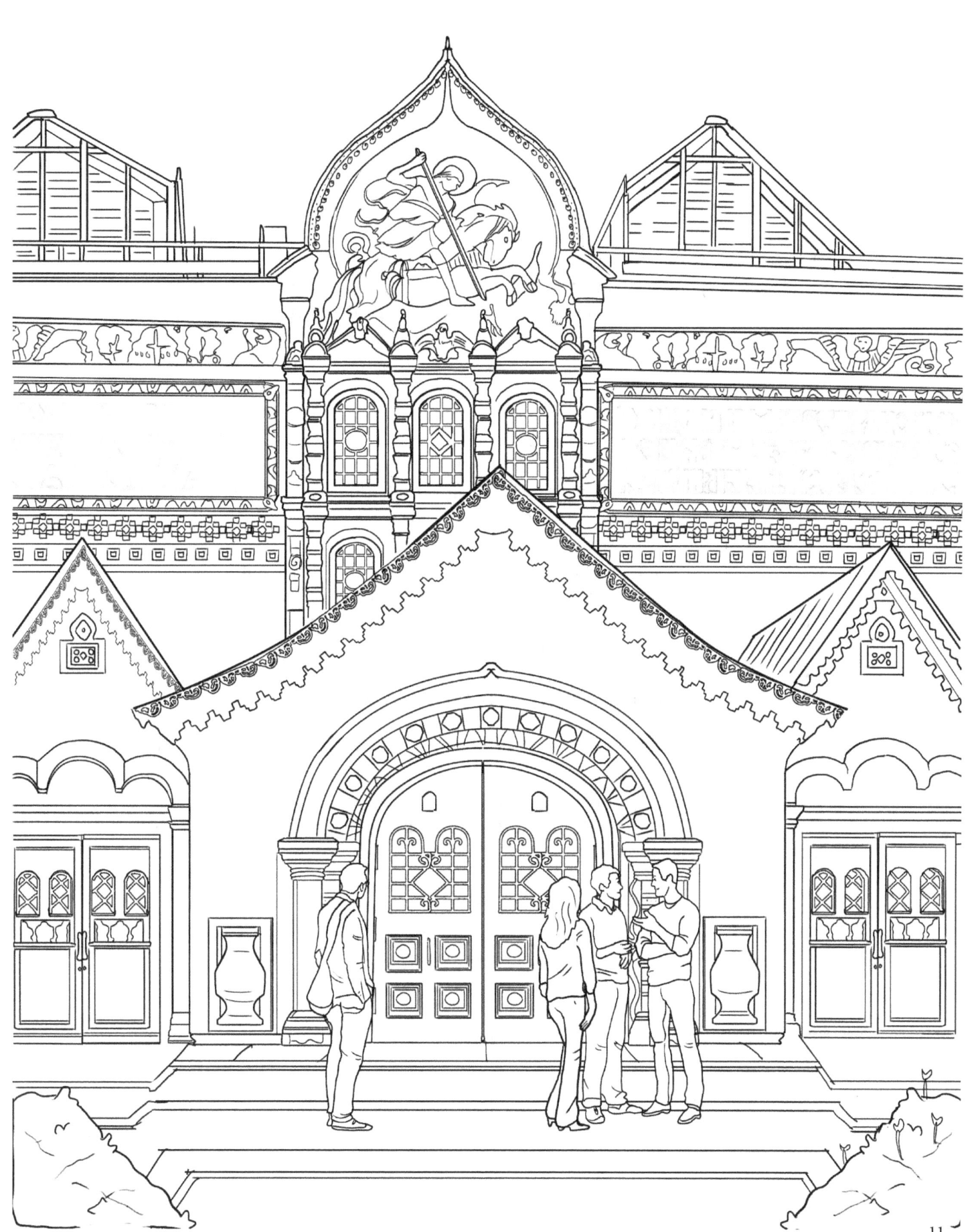

11

Plate 5.
Tretyakov Gallery

The State Tretyakov Gallery houses the biggest collection of Russian art in the world; it includes works of art spanning a period of a thousand years.

The gallery was founded by a Moscow merchant and patron of the arts, Pavel Tretyakov, who acquired a number of works by Russian artists of his day in the 1850s. He supported the famous "Peredvizhniki" movement. The Peredvizhnhiki, sometimes called "The Wanderers" or "The Itinerants" in English, were a group of like-minded artists who refused to conform to academic rules and restrictions and wanted their art to be a realistic representation of contemporary life in Russia. Tretyakov's desire was to create a collection of valuable national art that could grow into a museum. He bought an impressive number of paintings by Russian artists such as Vasily Perov, Ivan Kramskoi, Ilya Repin, Vasily Surikov, Isaak Levitan and Valentin Serov. In 1892 Tretyakov donated his collection of approximately two thousand works including paintings, sculptures and drawings, to the Russian nation.

The main building of the gallery is located in Moscow's Lavrushinsky Lane. Its world-famous front was designed by the Russian painter Viktor Vasnetsov who drew his inspiration from Russian fairytales. The Gallery's building on Krymsky Val (The New Tretyakov Gallery) was opened in 1983. It now houses the only permanent exhibition of the 20th century Russian art in the country, displaying avant-garde masterpieces by Kazimir Malevich, Vasily Kandinsky, Mark Chagall, Pavel Filonov and many others.

The gallery's collection of Russian art is continuously expanding. It now contains more than 130,000 exhibits — icons, paintings, graphics and sculpture — ranging from Andrei Rublev's "Trinity" to Kazimir Malevich's "Black Square". It is no wonder that, each year, the Tretyakov Gallery attracts more than a million visitors from Russia and from around the world.

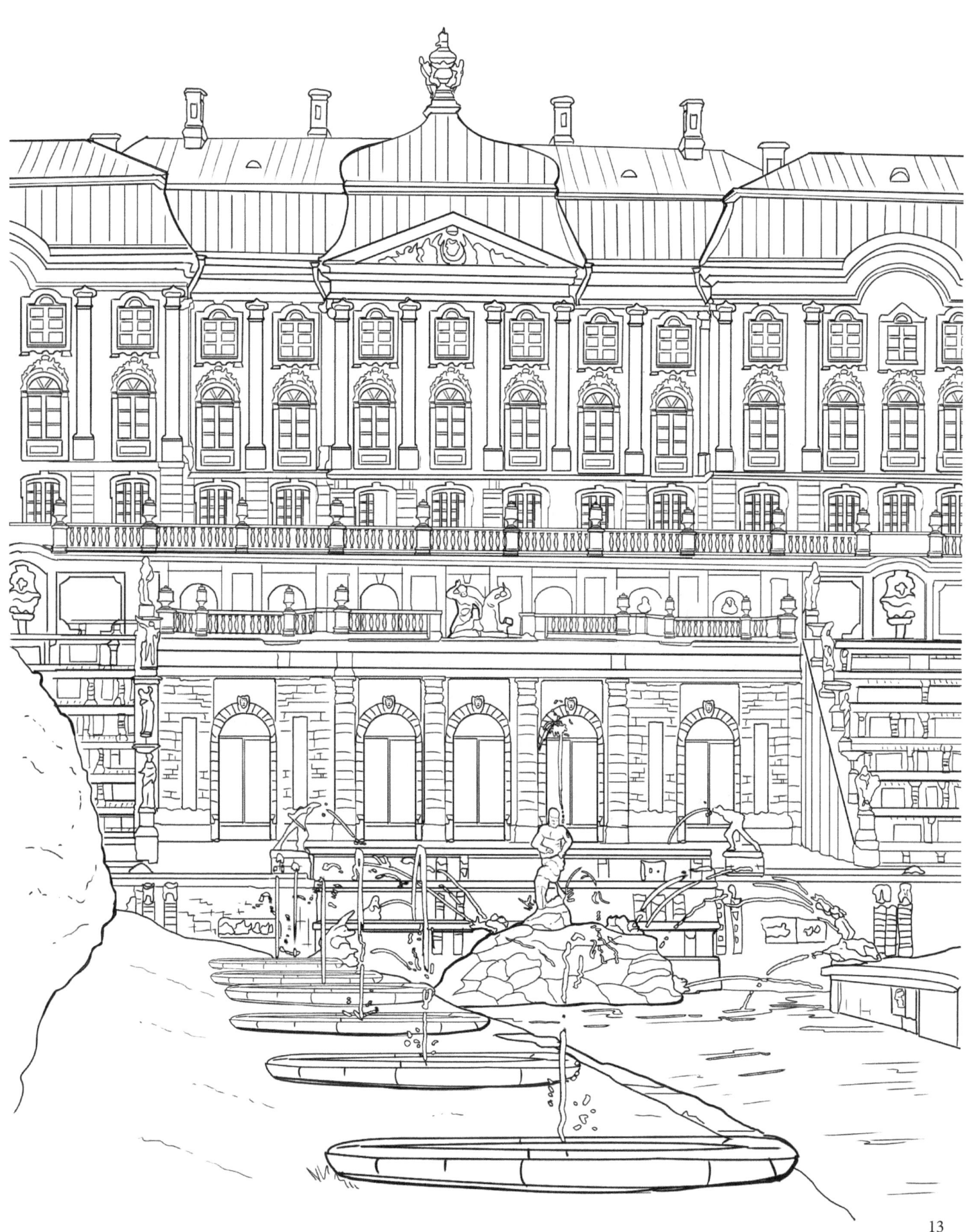

Plate 6.
Peterhof Palace

The architectural ensemble of Peterhof is one of Saint Petersburg's most famous attractions and a part of a UNESCO World Heritage Site. Peterhof, meaning "Peter's Court" in German, is sometimes referred to as "The Russian Versailles." It was indeed inspired by the French palace of Versailles and it was built to fulfill Peter the Great's desire to have a spectacular imperial palace in the suburbs of his new city.

The Grand Palace, the largest of Peterhof's group of palaces, is the centerpiece of the architectural ensemble. Designed by the French architect Jean-Baptiste Le Blond, the building was completed in 1721. Peter, however, had another palace built for himself in Peterhof — a smaller and less luxurious Monplaisir, that later became his preferred retreat.

When Peter's daughter Elizabeth came to the throne, Peterhof's parks, gardens and fountains were greatly improved. She also commissioned the Italian architect Bartolomeo Rastrelli to expand the Grand Palace, and it acquired its present-day appearance. The palace's interior is lavish and elegant, with an incredibly ornate ceremonial staircase as well as luxuriously decorated rooms featuring unique design elements, beautiful paintings, frescos and fine parquet floors.

Another famous Peterhof landmark is the spectacular ensemble of fountains, "Grand Cascade", running from the Grand Palace to the Marine Canal. It consists of 64 different fountains, 200 bronze statues and other decorations. At the center of the composition is Rastrelli's statue of Samson prizing open the jaws of a lion, symbolizing Russia's victory in The Great Northern War (the lion is an element of the Swedish coat of arms, and one of the most notable victories of the war took place on St. Samson's Day).

Amongst the other Peterhof fountains are mafnificent ensembles like "The Chess Cascade" and "The Pyramid Fountain." It is also worth mentioning the so-called "Joke Fountains": stepping on a certain stone activates them and everyone around gets soaked, thanks to Peter the Great's sense of humor.

During World War II Peterhof was captured by German troops and was largely destroyed, but the restoration work was initiated as soon as the war was over.

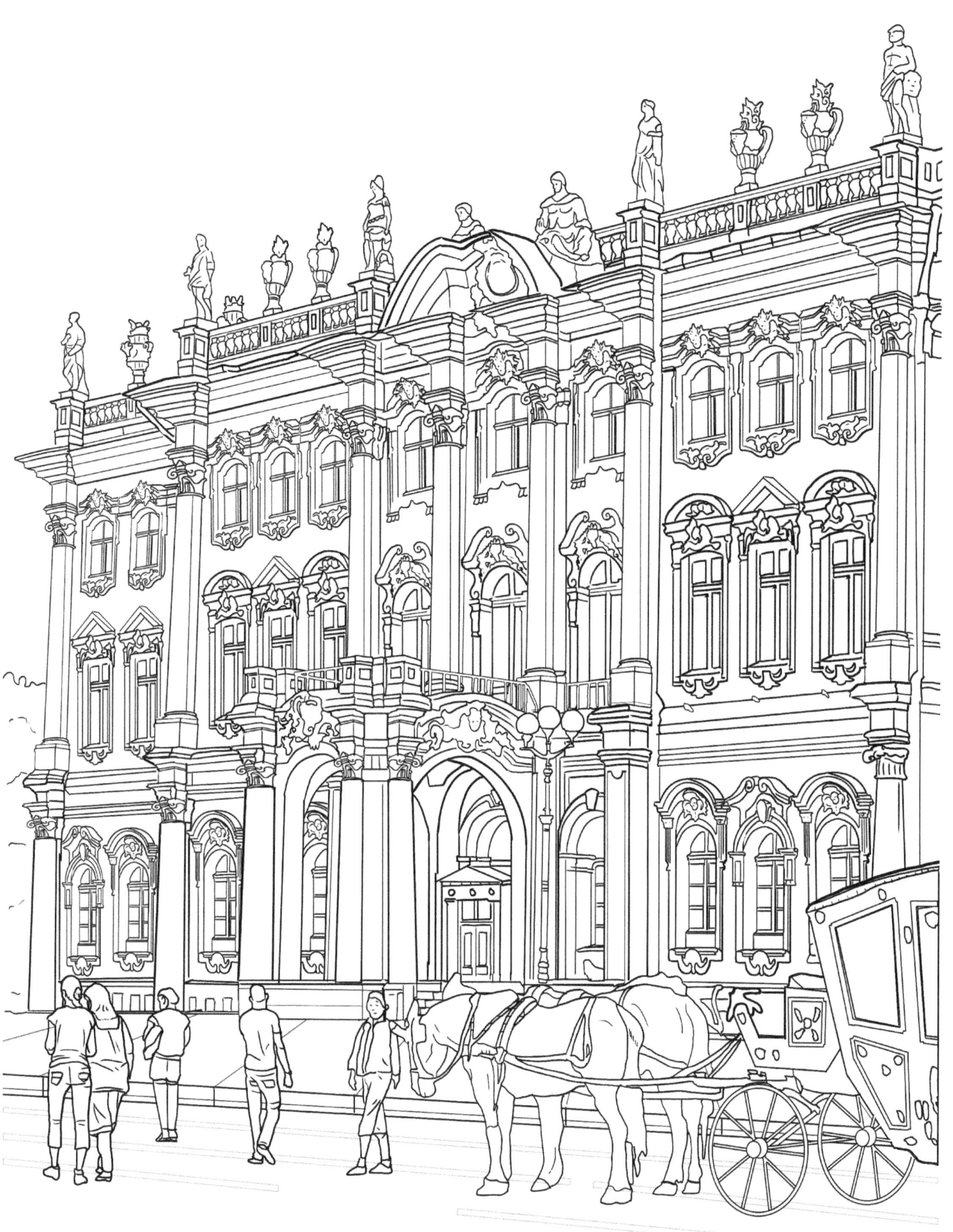

Plate 7.
Hermitage Museum

The Hermitage Museum in Saint Petersburg is one of the largest and oldest museums in the world. It was founded in 1764 by Catherine the Great and has been open to the public since 1852. The museum's incredibly rich and diverse collection comprises about three million items, with only a small part of these treasures being on permanent display. The major exhibition occupies six historic buildings along the Palace Embankment, including the impressive Winter Palace, a former official residence of Russian monarchs.

The Hermitage was founded by Catherine the Great who acquired numerous works of art from European aristocrats. Catherine's collection was initially meant for her own enjoyment; it was displayed in remote rooms of the palace, that is how it got the name "Hermitage", derived from Old French "hermit" meaning "recluse". The collection was embellished by each of Catherine's successors and immensely enhanced by Bolsheviks' confiscations. The Hermitage's treasures range from ancient Siberian artifacts to post-impressionist masterpieces by Van Gogh, Picasso and Matisse. Equally remarkable are the voluptuously decorated State Rooms of the Winter Palace.

According to estimates, it would take eleven years to view each exhibit for just one minute, which makes it impossible to appreciate everything that is on display. It is best to come prepared and look for the parts of the collection you are interested in!

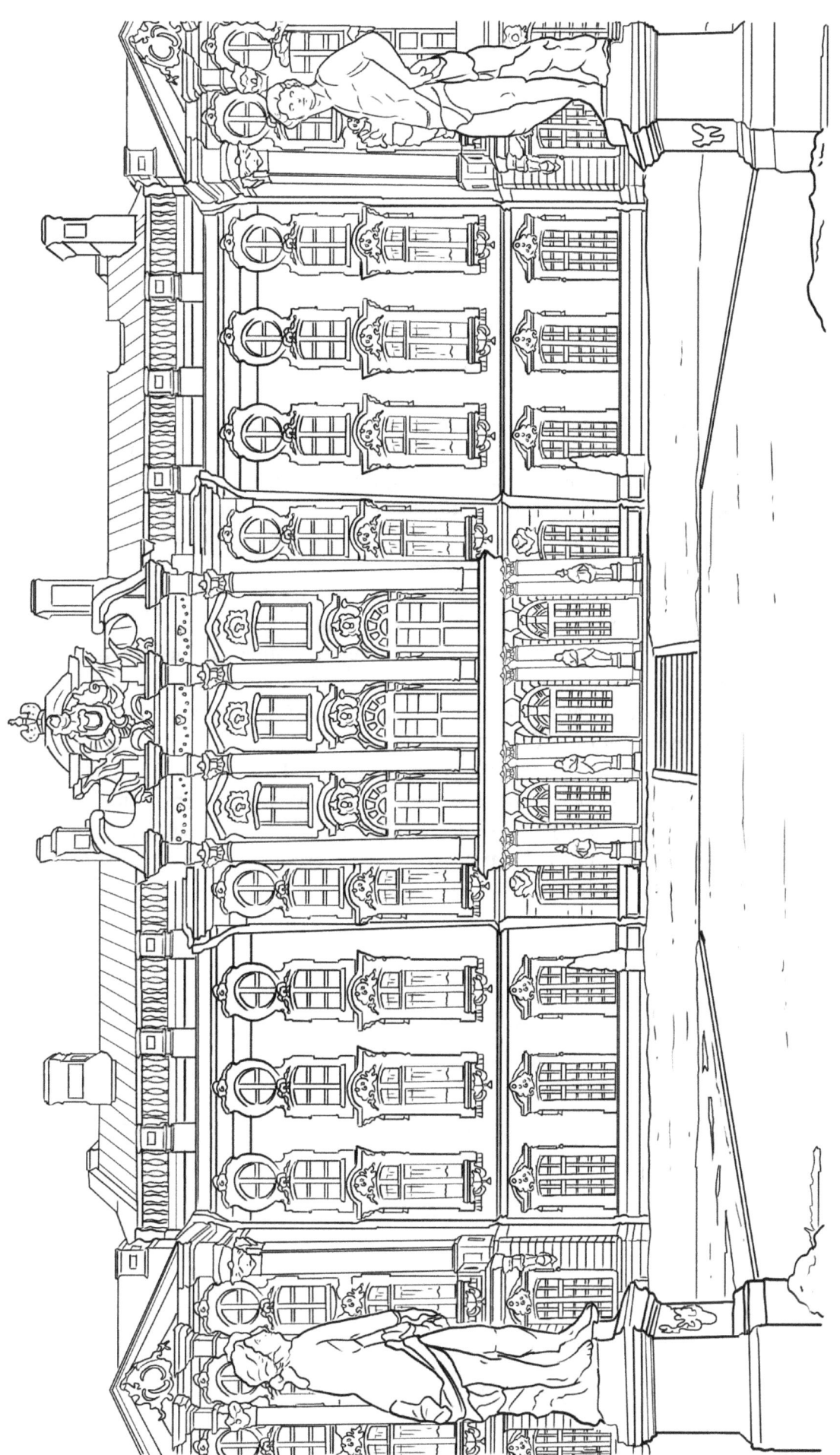

Plate 8.
Catherine Palace

Built for Empress Elizabeth by the renowned Italian architect Bartholomeo Rastrelli, the Catherine Palace became the summer residence of the Russian Tsars. It is situated in Tsarskoe Selo, 30 km south of Saint Petersburg. The enormous and luxurious palace, decorated with blue and white facades featuring gilded atlantes, caryatids and pilasters, was completed in 1756. Its exteriors required more than 100 kg of gold!

The interiors of the Catherine Palace are even more spectacular. The Great Hall occupies nearly 1000 square meters, offering magnificent views from its large arched windows. The walls are adorned with an impressive quantity of gilded stucco and the entire ceiling is covered by a monumental fresco entitled "The Triumph of Russia".

The highlights of the palace also include "The Great Staircase" with ornate banisters and reclining marble cupids and "The White Dining Room" that features a beautiful traditional blue-and-white tiled stove. Amongst the other significant rooms are "The Portrait Hall," which contains striking portraits of both Catherine and Elizabeth, and "The Picture Gallery" with exquisite 17th and 18th century canvases. However, the biggest attention is drawn to the legendary "Amber Room", an extraordinary chamber covered with panels of amber mosaic, gilded carving, mirrors and gemstones from the Ural Mountains and the Caucasus. In 1941, when German troops captured Tsarskoe Selo, "The Amber Room" was dismantled; the eventual fate of the original panels is still unknown. The process of the renovation took over 20 years and cost more that $12 million.

ABOUT THE BOOK

Explore Russia's greatest landmarks through this coloring book. From enigmatic St. Basil's Cathedral to the majestic Peterhof Palace, this book is perfect for any lover of Russian culture.

This page intentionally left blank.

www.ingramcontent.com/pod-product-compliance
Lightning Source LLC
Chambersburg PA
CBHW081307170526
45165CB00010B/3286